I0162479

Fortune Cookies

Volume 5

Dr. Kareem Pottinger

YSD Publishing House

Library of Congress Catalog in Publication Data

Copyright 2007 by KAREEM POTTINGER

All rights reserved. No portion of this book may be reproduced, By any process or technique, without the express written consent of the publisher.

YSD PUBLISHING HOUSE
14490 Coastal Bay Circle 13204
Naples, FL. 34119

Library of Congress Catalog Card Number:
2013934185
International Standard Book Number 978-1-937171-04-9

Dedicated to my firstborn

YOUNGSABATH POTTINGER

If I ever leave this planet, I have
always kept you in mind.

Not leavening my wisdom far behind

Grow Good

INTRODUCTION

The true intent of this book
was to write a set of guidelines
that could be
immediately implemented in
the progress and advancement
of my sons elite
life.
This vast deep knowledge was
to be used as a
tool
to keep him far beyond just,
"ahead of the learning curb" for
lack of better expression.
These
rules are the widely accepted
and used unspoken
secrets amongst the elite in
which we use to rear our

young.
Although these are our
secrets
and most of us will and should
be extremely displeased for
having them on display for the
"normal's" of the world to
receive, I decided to release
them nevertheless.
For,
upon reading the finished
piece I realized that these elite
secrets
could not only serve to benefit
my son and family to come
well, but that the entire
world
could serve to benefit from
these lists of guidelines.
The way that this book is
intended to be received is to

ponder upon each page for a complete 24 hours.

Each page is to be pondered upon for the whole day; it is to be used as topic of discussion for that day amongst peers, friends, and family members' etcetera.

It is especially designed to be pondered upon mostly by you. For a complete 24 hours deep thought on each subject should be pondered upon. The reason being is to see how these guidelines could be implemented into your current life, how should they have been implemented in your past life, and how can they benefit your future.

It
is only through the true
belief
and usage of these
guidelines
that your life's
works will be greatly
affected
in its progress.

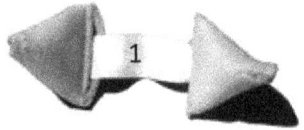

In life; you should live everyday to the fullest because it is never certain that tomorrow will come for anyone of us

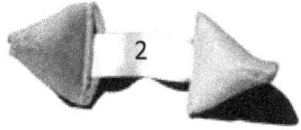

The
worst
punishment
happens
to
those
that
squander-off
their
good
fortunes

When you are
engineering
your
steps
it is
extremely
important
to make sure
that your
start link
is a
success

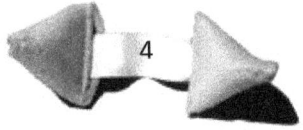

Doing;
is
the
wisdom
of
knowing

Your lifestyle
has to
match with
where you
would like
to
end-up
or
you will
never
end-up
there

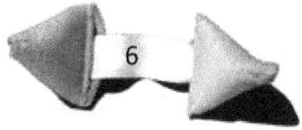

*You should
always
try
to
maximize
the
amount
of
time
you have
on
good-run*

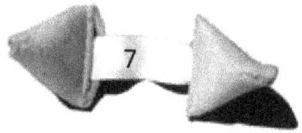

*You can
get
everything
you want
in
life
when you
are
willing to
work
for
it*

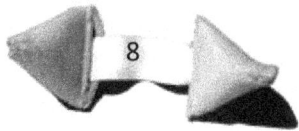

*When
the
coconut
falls,
make
sure that
you
are
not
underneath
the
tree*

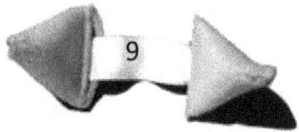

*Upset
should
never
go
before
the
cause
and
the
effect*

In conversation;
if
you are not
hurting or
helping
an individual,
then
you
really
are
not
saying
anything

*Everything
that
happens in life
happens how it
is set-up
to happen; and
the sooner that
you realize this
fact, the more
control you will
have over your
life*

You have to feed
the
people
ice cream
on
Sunday
if you want them
to go to
war
for
you
on
Monday

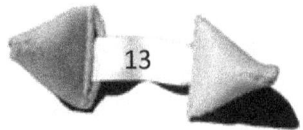

*In life what
counts
is
not how
you
start a thing
but
the way
that
you
finish
that thing*

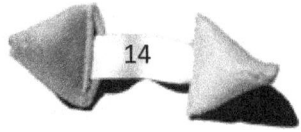

*To always be
hedging
your
bets
will give
you
more
of a
direct-route
towards
your
success*

*When
people resort
to
lying,
it is
to
keep
things
on
an
even
level*

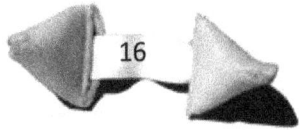

Never dwell upon the things that you cannot change, for it will be a waste of your precious-time but in its stead look for the opportunities that you can create

*In order to
alleviate the
initial offset;
telling people
what they want
to hear
and then doing
what you want,
is a
technique that
should work for
you*

For
the
just of
your
cause
you
should
be
willing
to
risk-it
all

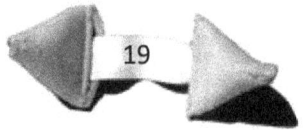

Being careful about your wants will take care of your needs

*Don't ever
confuse
trying as a
goal,
the whole point
of trying is to
achieve*

*so
achieving
would be the
goal of
trying*

*You cannot
help
anyone-else
unless
you help
yourself first
and to help
someone-else
before helping
yourself is
doing you both
a disservice*

*Sometimes
you may have
to do
what you
do not
want to do
in order
to
get
what
you
want*

*You should
never
place your trust
in
people
but
rather
place your
trust
in
the
moment*

*Always
focus
on
achieving
your
purpose
and
your
agenda
will
be
fulfilled*

*You have
to at least
swing
the
bat
in
order
to
hit
the
ball*

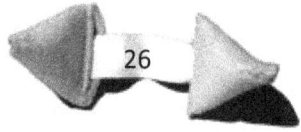

The difference between a genius and the average person is; the genius always knows why they are there at the place their at and the latter does not

The choices that you have made in your life has determined the situation that you are currently in

*In every
problem
there
is a
hidden
opportunity,
look
for-it
and
you
will
find-it*

Because there is always room for improvement in everyone's life; in order to better yourself, you should always strive to be more than you are at this present-moment

*You should
always
shoot-holes
into the
things
that you are
involved in
in order to
make sure
that they
are
bullet- proof*

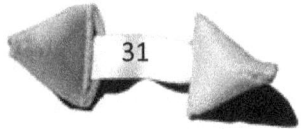

*You have to be
observant
of the
turbulence
when you make
your way
to the
top
because it is
windy
all the way up
there*

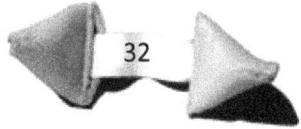

*It is important
to
understand
the
fact that the
rules
can always
change
depending
on
who is using
them*

*Nothing great
that
you
will
accomplish
will
ever
happen
without
sacrifice*

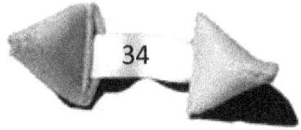

*Always
remember that
the
world
moves
for
love,
it
bows-down
before
it*

Never become
a product of
your
environment
but
let
the
environment
become
a
product
of
you

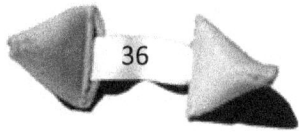

*There will
always
be
someone-else
in this
life
who
is
smarter
that you
can
learn from*

*In anything
that
you do, your
pace
will be
a
huge
determining
factor
of
your
success*

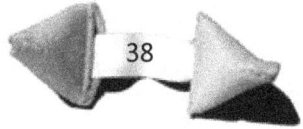

*It is important
to understand
that what is
easy
for another
may not be
easy
for you and
what is easy
for you may not
be easy for
another*

The one who is in charge, their list of things to do is a lot heavier than the average person's list of things to do

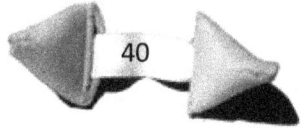

*A bone
is just a
bone
until one
lion
tells
the
other
lion
they are
leaving
with
it*

What

was

once

true

then

will

always

be

true

now

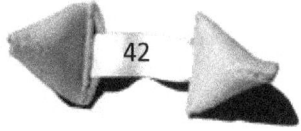

*Keep your
eyes-open
for your
acquisitions
but
for your
friends
keep
them
open
even
bigger*

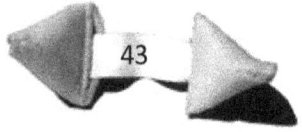

*It
does not
matter
what
you use
to get
the
job-done
after the
fact
that you have
already gotten
the job-done*

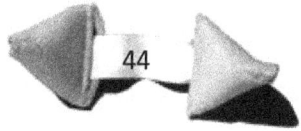

As soon as you
realize that a
thing
is not
working-out,
you need to
take
the
initiative
to
end
it

*After
conquest
should
always
come
construction*

*Find
something
meaningful
to do
with your
life
and
you will
feel
better
about
yourself*

*It is important
to understand
that when you
dance
with a
devil,
that
devil
does not
change but
instead
you will*

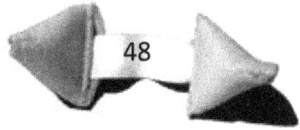

*In life everyone
does get a
chance
to
become
outstanding,
you just have
to be able
to realize that
this is the
chance
in order for you
to take it*

*In life;
half
measures mean
absolutely
nothing,
either
you go
full-blast
or
not
at
all*

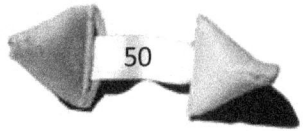

*In
the
absence
of
light
darkness
will
always
prevails*

*In whatever
job
you do;
if you
strive
to do your
best,
good luck will
follow
you around
in
that
job*

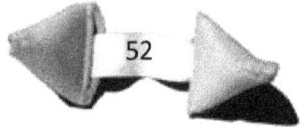

We

as

human-beings

get

properly

trained

through

our

mistakes

53

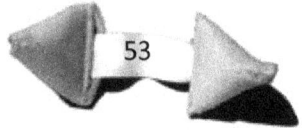

Life
is
a
responsibility
that
will
deal
with
your
actions

54

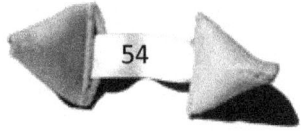

When
your
life
becomes
hard
you
will
just
have
to
hit
harder

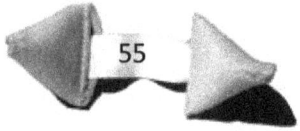

*A
person who
invest
is
a
person
who
is
going
to
have
success*

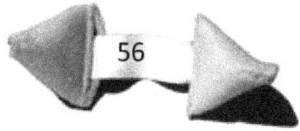

*Life
is
all
about
your
memories
so
get out there
and
go make
some
wonderful-ones*

*In whatever it
is
that you
are
doing
you should
always
leave
room
for
correcting
mistakes*

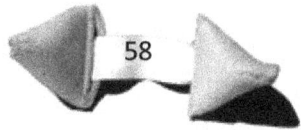

*There should
never
be any
worries
when you
possess
real-talent
because
it
will always
shine
through*

*People
do
many
different
things
for
a
wide-variety
of
reasons*

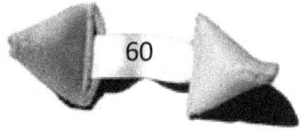

Sometimes
you
will
have
to
stoop-down
low
in
order
to
conquer

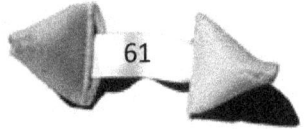

*The
one-way
to
never
give-up
on
your dreams
is to
always be
doing
something
about them*

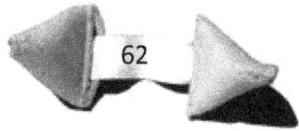

Sometimes
you will have to
go
through
the
whole list
of
ideas
before you
get
one
right

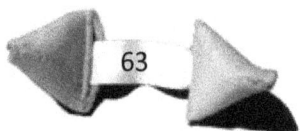

When you take a five minute pause to think about what you are going to do, you will never have to worry about running around like a headless-chicken

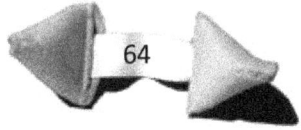

*Succeeding
in a
great-way
will
always come
down
to
who can
improvise,
adapt,
and
overcome*

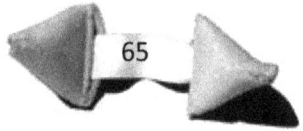

*The more
control
you have
in
whatever
it is
that you
are
doing
will always be
the better
for you*

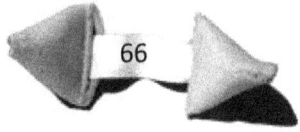

There are choices in life, with every choice that you make there are consequences and this is extremely important for you to understand

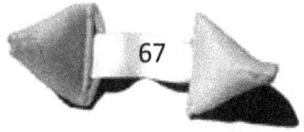

*One
of
the
secrets
to
success
in
anything
is
drive
and
persistence*

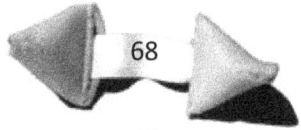

*Lose any ugly
attitudes that
you may
possess
because when
you posses
an
ugly-attitude
it just makes
you
appear
ugly*

*True character
exists
when one
learns
from their
mistakes,
picks
themselves
up,
and
presses
on*

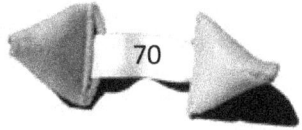

*You can
tell
someone's
true-character
by
the
way
they
decide
to
end
things*

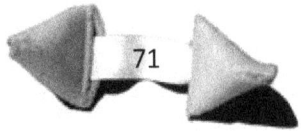

*When you know
that you are
living and
walking in the
most highest of
plans, then take
comfort
in
knowing
that you will
always
be more than
alright*

*When
you face
big-problems,
there
is nothing
that
you can do
but to
get
busy
fixing
them*

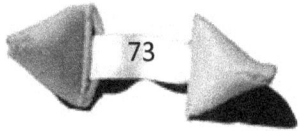

*When
you break-up
with
someone,
you
break-up
with
a part
of
that
person's
life*

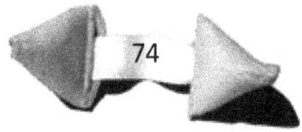

Sometimes

you

just

have

to

wait

for

it

*The
Universe
will
only
help
those
that
help
themselves*

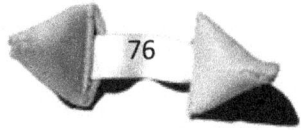

You
have
to
train your
brain
to be one;
either
a
winner
or
a
loser

*When you
would like
to keep your
dream
alive; besides
the work that
you are doing
towards your
dream,
you have to
go to the
top-people*

Call
an
audible
when
you
see
that
the
original-plans
are
not
working

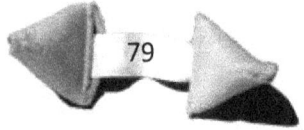

*Be careful
when you
do
the
wrong
things
because
you
will
pay
the
price*

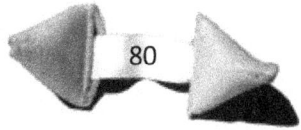

*If
you
cannot
afford
new
tires
then
get
used
ones*

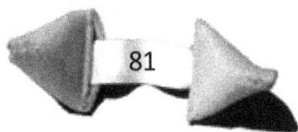

*You
will
never
need
to
get
ready
if
you
stay
ready*

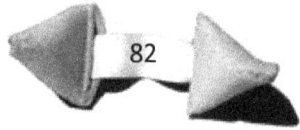

*It is important
to
understand
that when you
are getting
left-behind
and you would
like to
keep-up,
you have to
move a little bit
faster*

*You
never really
know
yourself
until
you
sit-down
and
talk
to
someone
else*

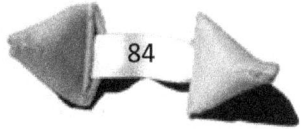

You will never
be able to help
the fact
that you are
who you
are
and the only
thing that you
can do about it,
is to train
yourself to
become better

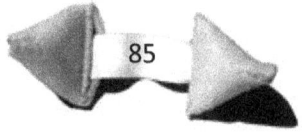

Part
of
maturity
is
having
a
conflict
and
learning
from
it

Nothing
ever
goes
exactly
as
planned
so
don't
get
dismayed
when
things don't

The moment
that you
become
embarrassed
with
who you are, is
the
very moment
that
you
lose
yourself

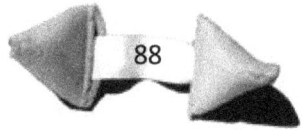

*It is important
to
remember
that it is
only when
you take
a
step-back
that you
can
see the
entire-view*

Understand
that
when
you
cannot
keep-up,
you
get
left
behind

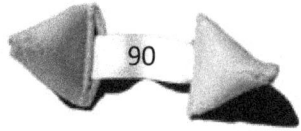

*Negative-people
attract
negative-things
towards
their
lives,
which is why
it is
important
to stay
far-away
from them*

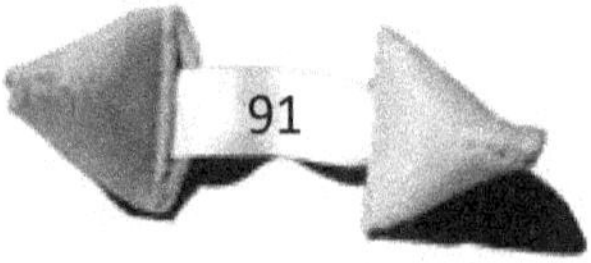

*Never
hate
your
advisory
because
it
will
always
affect
your
judgment*

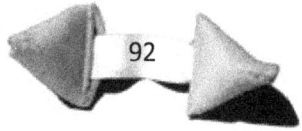

Perfection cannot be rushed

*If
it
does
not
make
sense
then
most
likely
it
is
not
true*

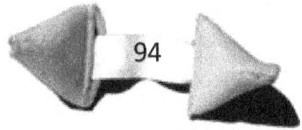

It is an extreme waste of your time to try an teach an ignorant-person what you perceive as right because they are going to do what they are going to do regardless

*To
have
any
kind
of
success
you
have
to
take
action*

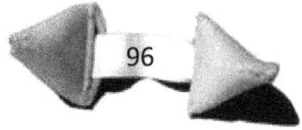

*You
can
always
show
what
but
never
show
how*

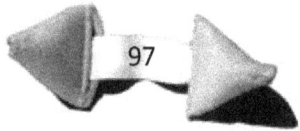

*You
cannot
achieve
success
unless
you
are
properly
trained*

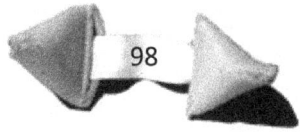

*Because
you have
done a thing
does
not
mean
that you
have
to
continue
doing
that thing*

*Money
is not
as
valuable
to an
organization
as knowing
who to
place
your
confidence
in*

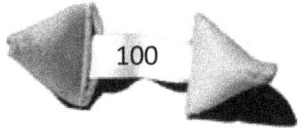

*In
life
you
should
try
to
create
a lot
of
choices
for
yourself*

*The people
who
insist
on giving
advice
are usually
the same
ones
who
never
take
it*

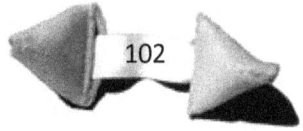

*Do not ever be
so
focused
on
your
enemies
that you
forget
to
watch
your
friends*

Do not chase what you cannot catch

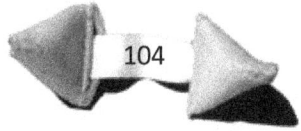

*Geniuses
are
geniuses
because
their
moves
are
always
calculated*

*There are
two types of
people
in this
world;
those
that
want to do
and
those that
actually
do*

Do not ever let yourself be controlled by fear, being controlled by fear is a weak-minded persons game

*Those
that
hesitate,
lose*

*Be wary
of
having
liars
around
you
because
successful
cover-ups
become
second
nature*

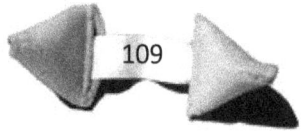

*Your
dreams
are your
ticket
out
of
whatever
situation
you
are
currently
in*

*No
one
in
life
ever
got
ahead
by
sitting
on
their
behind*

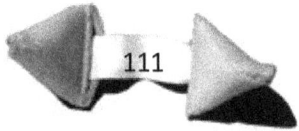

*Defeat
by
a
small
margin
will
always
allow
that
defeat
to
linger*

*Even though
you have
shaken
every
tree,
if you have
one
idea
left
you
should not
give-up*

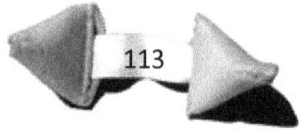

*It is only by
living
on the edge
that we as
human-beings
will
find out
who we
truly
are underneath
our
skin*

There should be no more room for good in your life when you are searching for greatness

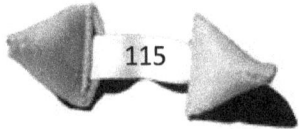

*It is not only
important
the decisions
that you
choose
to make but
also
the ones
that
you
do
not*

*In
order
to
have a
new
beginning
something
else
in your
life
has to
end*

*Power
tends
to
wear-out
the
ones
without
it*

*The
person
who
builds
upon
people
ultimately
builds
upon
mud*

Things
will
always
be
easier
to
find
when
they
are
stuck
together

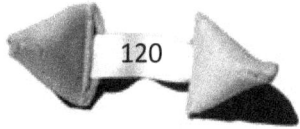

*Just because
you have made
it to the
finals
does not
mean
that you
should
forget
about
the
championship*

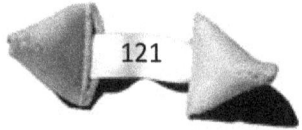

*You
will
always
be
remembered
by
your
first
impression*

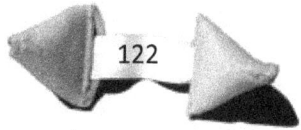

You never have
to
speak
when
your work is
great
because
your work will
always
speak
for
itself

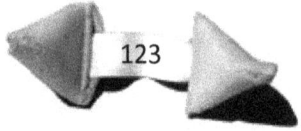

*Do not allow
yourself
to be
placed
into
scary
situations
and
you will not be
placed
into scary
situations*

*Life
is
always
happening
all around
us
all the
time; it
does not
stop for you
or
anyone else*

*It is important to
understand
that
options
are
advantages
and
the more
options
that you have,
the more
advantages
you have*

*It is very
important to get
the use out of
the things that
you now
have because
once lost
it takes
twice the effort
to get
them
back*

When
certain-things
pop-up
that is not a
part of your
master-plan
it is
important to
realize that not
all things in life
you can
control

*You should
always
make
the most
of the
time
that
you
have
left
in this
life*

*If you should
learn
anything; it is
that you should
have
the people
that
love you around
you for as
long
as
you can*

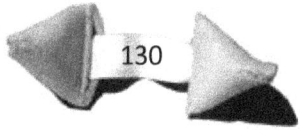

In order to expand on the wealth that you are trying to create, you have to take on superior strategies that is equivalent to the wealth that you are trying to create

*An
unjust-way
of
how
to
live
will
ultimately
destroys
itself*

It is extremely important to think through and to truly know that you want to do what you are attempting to do,
before you actually start to do it

*Be careful
of
trying to do too
much
when you only
need to do a
little
in order
to
win
the
game*

Once
hit
hard
enough
all
bullies
will
back
down

The
best
time
to
stop
a
altercation
is
before
it
happens

Any spouse wants a person that they can turn to

*When you
make
a
decision
on
what
you
see
and
it
doesn't
work-out;
move-on*

*Drama
is
conflict; you
should not
put-up
or
deal with it,
just
option
not be
around
it at all*

By pointing your life in a certain direction; you will live and make of it the most that you can but at some-point your fated destiny will kick-in

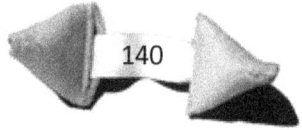

One of the many secrets to success is image, how you appear to the outside-world

is

exactly

how the outside-world will treat you

*You will pay
the
price
for
making
a
mistake,
everyone
in
this
world
does*

*It
will
always
be
an
excellent
idea
for you
to
elevate
your
perfection*

It is extremely important for your self-esteem to always try things your way first and then if you do not succeed, you seek help to figure-out what you were doing wrong

When you have never done a thing; you can never truly know that thing regardless of how good someone else has described their experience of that thing to you

A

person's

reputation

will

always

contribute

to

their

success

or

take away

from it

*Know
how
to
change
and
you will
know
and
see
growth
within
yourself*

Don't ever give-up on yourself; any task that you cannot do alone, you will be able to do with the help of others

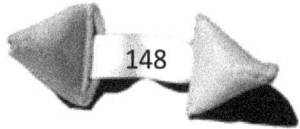

*You have to
feel
beautiful
and
happy
in
order
to
be
beautiful
and
happy*

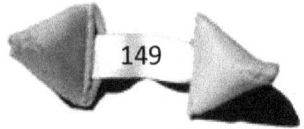

*It is
important
to
learn
how
to
live
life
according
to
life's
rules*

When your advisory's are making mistakes it is important for you not to interrupt them

The unknown
is
scary for
most-people
which
is why the
majority of the
people in the
world get stuck
in a rut; do not
aspire to be like
them

*It is important
for you
to
understand
that
whatever you
do not allow to
be done to
you,
cannot be
done
unto you*

*Not
having
your
time
management
down
can
really
harm
you
in
the end*

When
people come on
your job
telling
other
people what
to
do,
it
lessons
your
authority

*Determination
means
that
you
will do
whatever
it is
you
have to do
in order
to
succeed*

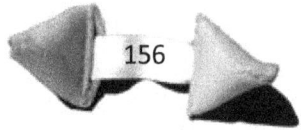

In dealing with success; it is important to diversify,

you
should not
like to put
all your
eggs
into
that
one-basket

*A
tailspin
is
extremely
hard
to
pull-out
of,
do not
put
yourself
into one of them*

*You should
never
show
anything
until
it
is
completely
ready
to
be
shown*

The end

Additional books written by
Dr. Kareem Pottinger available online at
www.FORTUNECOOKIES.me
and your local book stores nationwide
FORTUNE COOKIES VOLUMES 1-11

also   available   on   your

Kindle   Nook   Apple   devices

  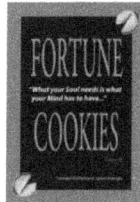

www.ingramcontent.com/pod-product-compliance
Lightning Source LLC
Chambersburg PA
CBHW030104070426
42448CB00037B/960

ÉTUDE CROISÉE DES CONCEPTS: LINGUISTIQUE, INTERCULTURALITÉ ET SOCIOLINGUISTIQUE: VALEURS, LIMITES ET PERSPECTIVES

~

CROSSOVER STUDY OF CONCEPTS: LINGUISTICS, INTERCULTURALITY AND SOCIOLINGUISTICS: VALUES, LIMITS AND PERSPECTIVES

~

CROSSOVER STUDIE DER KONZEPTE: LINGUISTIK, INTERKULTURALITÄT UND SOZIOLINGUISTIK: WERTE, GRENZEN UND AUSSICHTEN

Dr. Jean René MAFFO

© Jean René MAFFO
Professor and writer
Phone:(+49)1521838278I
Email: jean.rene.maffo2016@gmail.com
Kendenicher Strasse 85
Hurth-Germany

The rights of Jean René Maffo to be identified as the author of this work have been asserted by him in accordance with the Copyright, Designs and Patents Act of 1988.
All rights reserved; no part of this publication may be reproduced, stored in a retrieval system, or transmitted in any form or by any means, electronic, mechanical, photocopying, recording or otherwise without the prior written consent of the publisher or a licence permitting copying in the UK issued by the Copyright Licensing Agency Ltd, www.cla.co.uk

ISBN 978-1-78222-606-2

Book design, layout and production management by Into Print www.intoprint.net, +44 (0)1604 832140